YOUR KNOWLEDGE HAS VALUE

- We will publish your bachelor's and master's thesis, essays and papers

- Your own eBook and book - sold worldwide in all relevant shops

- Earn money with each sale

Upload your text at www.GRIN.com
and publish for free

Bibliographic information published by the German National Library:

The German National Library lists this publication in the National Bibliography; detailed bibliographic data are available on the Internet at http://dnb.dnb.de .

This book is copyright material and must not be copied, reproduced, transferred, distributed, leased, licensed or publicly performed or used in any way except as specifically permitted in writing by the publishers, as allowed under the terms and conditions under which it was purchased or as strictly permitted by applicable copyright law. Any unauthorized distribution or use of this text may be a direct infringement of the author s and publisher s rights and those responsible may be liable in law accordingly.

Imprint:

Copyright © 2011 GRIN Verlag, Open Publishing GmbH
Print and binding: Books on Demand GmbH, Norderstedt Germany
ISBN: 978-3-668-14767-6

This book at GRIN:

http://www.grin.com/en/e-book/195455/the-300-movie-vs-the-historical-300-at-thermopylae-real-historical

Star Smith

The "300" Movie vs. the Historical 300 at Thermopylae. Real Historical Facts and Narrative Fact Based Stories

GRIN Publishing

GRIN - Your knowledge has value

Since its foundation in 1998, GRIN has specialized in publishing academic texts by students, college teachers and other academics as e-book and printed book. The website www.grin.com is an ideal platform for presenting term papers, final papers, scientific essays, dissertations and specialist books.

Visit us on the internet:

http://www.grin.com/

http://www.facebook.com/grincom

http://www.twitter.com/grin_com

More than Meets the Eye:

300 Movie VS. Real Battle of Thermopylae

Honors History paper on Real Historical Facts VS. Narrative Fact based stories

"The events are ninety percent accurate...I've shown this movie to world-class historians who have said it's amazing. They can't believe it's as accurate as it is." stated Zack Snyder director of the movie *300*, based on the historical battle of Thermopylae. Albeit, the movie does have a lot of truth to it, it also has many fallacies. It is true that there was an epic battle at Thermopylae where King Leonidas of Sparta took 300 soldiers, all with a male heir at home, into the 'Hot Gates' where they held the Persian army at bay for three days. Xerxes did have an army of 10,000 men called the Immortals. A man name Ephialtes did betray Greece by showing Xerxes men through the Anopaia path allowing them to surround the Greek forces. At the age of seven, young boys were taken away from their parents and sent to the Agoge in order to become a Hoplite soldier. Even with the minor truths portrayed in the movie; upon deeper inspection of the history of Thermopylae, it becomes apparent that the movie is nowhere near ninety percent accurate. The genre of the film itself is 'fiction.' It was not made to be a 'documentary.' Therefore, to make the assertion Mr. Snyder made is misleading the audience to believe that the filmmaker's interpretation of the history of Thermopylae is fact. When in truth, the film loosely portrays the history of the battle and ends up being nothing more than pure entertainment.

   The first fictional piece of this film is depicted in the very opening scene when the narrator discusses the 'discarding' of the boy if he were "sickly or misshapen" (Wenham, David). The massive pile of skulls that sit at the base of the ravine where the Elder stands atop of the mountain inspecting the baby symbolizes the bones of the 'discarded'. This act of throwing a baby off of the cliff is completely false. It is understood that films, even those based on true stories embellish the facts so as to engage the audience, but historically, "At birth a boy was inspected by the elders, and if he appeared too weakly for future military service, he was taken into the mountains and abandoned" (Columbia). However, this historical fact proves to be theoretical as there has yet to be any concrete proof to confirm that the Spartan babies were abandoned in the woods and certainly, no bones or skulls have ever been found of any of the 'discarded' children. This example of the opening scene shows some exaggeration on the part of the filmmakers, but it is a small misrepresentation of the truth; there are more important perversions that need to be addressed in the film *300*.

    While it is true that the character "Delios", the only surviving soldier of the battle of Thermopylae is narrating the film as he retells the events to the remaining warriors that will continue the campaign at Plataea. The fallacies of the film; regardless that the story is being told from the perspective of a 'narrators' point of view, are too grand not to refute. It is understood that people tend to stretch the truth when retelling of events in order to make the situation more impressive than it might have been. This concept may even allow the audience to accept the fallacies as entertainment, but to pass off the events as accurate is deceitful and careless on the part of the filmmakers.

    When Delios states to his eager brethren that "A beast approaches, it was king Leonidas himself who provoked it" (Wenham, David), the filmmakers maintain that the battle of Thermopylae was brought upon by King Leonidas' act of kicking a Persian Herald into a well. That is nowhere near historical fact. According to Ernle Bradford in his book *The Battle for the West- Thermopylae*, there was a Herald that was sent to Persia by *King Darius I* to seek Sparta's submission to Persia. The Herald requested a token of "earth and water', but was thrown down a well. Bradford states that there is evidence to suggest the discarding of the Herald actually occurred and the Spartan's, upon throwing the Persian Ambassador in the well said to the Herald, "get earth and water from down there" (Bradford, 31). Nevertheless, this act was not done by Leonidas or even during Xerxes rule, nor was it the cause of the Persian invasion. In fact, it kept Xerxes from sending Heralds to Sparta during his reign to ask for submission, as he did not trust the Spartan's to adhere to International law, which regarded the Heralds as 'sacred and inviolable' because they had already killed a Persian Ambassador.

    The Persian invasion and the Battle of Thermopylae began in 546 BCE when Persia conquered Lydia and all its subject states. All citizens were required to pay hefty taxes and serve in the Persian army. Aristagoras, a Tyrant placed in power by the Persians to rule Miletus, seeking change began a rebellion in 499 BCE. He requested the help of Sparta, but they declined. He then sought out the help of the Athens. They agreed to join forces and promised Aristagoras twenty ships for the battle. In 498 BCE, the Athenians conquered and burned Sardis, which was the capital of Lydia. Looking to punish Athenians for their part in the rebellion, in 490 BCE Darius I, Persian king and father of Xerxes invaded Greece. At the Battle of Marathon, ten thousand Athenian Hoplites slaughtered the Persian army causing Darius and his men to retreat back to their ships. Six thousand Persians were dead compared to just two hundred Greeks.

    This defeat was the precursor to the Persian invasion. According to the historian Herodotus, Mardonius convinced his cousin Xerxes to invade Greece. "Master, it is not fitting that they of Athens escape scot-free, after doing the Persians such great injury. Complete the work which thou hast now in hand, and then, when the pride of Egypt is brought low, lead an army against Athens" (Herodotus and Rawlinson, 263). This was a convincing argument, and it gave Xerxes an opportunity to complete unfinished family business by punishing the Athenians for their impedance in the rebellion at Marathon, but what really pushed Xerxes to take two hundred thousand or more Persian soldiers into Greece were two popular minerals, Silver and Gold. Mardonius advise Xerxes that there were mines in Greece waiting to be consumed.

    Word had spread of the Persian threat to Athens; they in turn requested the help of Sparta, Arcadia, Thespiae and other city-states to stand against the enemy. This alliance would prove to be a changing moment in Greece as most city-states fought amongst one another, especially Athens and Persia. These two dominant societies were constantly battling for complete control over Greece and all of its city-states. Sparta had previous wars with Messenia, Argolis, and Tegea, while Athens had previously attacked Thebes. Civil war was constant in Greece, but being that Xerxes wanted to add Greece to his empire the choice to come together to fight and put their own issues aside was necessary. The total number of soldiers that ventured into the 'Hot Gates' to face the Persian Army was 7000. During the battle, the alliance fell apart and most of the Greeks retreated except Leonidas and his men, but they were not the only group of men to stay, 700 Thespians willingly stayed behind and stood beside the 300 Spartans to fight the onslaught of Persians. There were also 400 Thebes still in attendance and, according to Herodotus, they were forced to stay and kept as Hostages by Leonidas, "very much against their will" (Herodotus and Rawlinson 314). The movie makes reference to the retreat and it also makes reference that a small number stayed behind to face the enemy. This small number is the 300 Spartans that the movie is based upon, hence the name 300. The movie, however, does not mention that the 700 Thespians willingly and 400 Thebes unwillingly stayed and risked their lives as well.

    The filmmakers glorify the battle of Thermopylae and make the Spartans out to be 'honorable' people. It is true that the Spartans were very diligent in regard to their military training and their stand at Thermopylae should be seen as courageous, but aside from that, Spartans were no more than barbaric people. For example, "When a man wanted to marry a woman in ancient Sparta, he abducted her forcefully and had her head shaved" (O'Conner, K). When the young males were sent to the Agoge, they were beaten severely on a daily basis. Some of the boys were killed in training. Also, they were fed such small portions that they were forced to go out and steal food. If they were caught they were beaten, but not because they stole the food, rather because they got caught. This type of brutal training was necessary to create strong Hoplite soldiers that would be ready to fight at a moment's notice.

    Spartan's felt the need to be ready for war because they were outnumbered 10 to 1 by a group of Messenians that lived amongst them. "The world will know that *free* men stood against a tyrant, that few stood against many, and before this battle was over, even a god-king can bleed." Stated king Leonidas to Xerxes in the film 300. A powerful statement that gripped the audience, but unfortunately it is false as well. The previous quote leads the audience to believe that Sparta was a state free of Slavery and that only 'free men' fought at the battle of Thermopylae, but that is entirely untrue. In 725 BCE, the Spartans conquered Messenia. The conquered people became "Agriculture" slaves for Sparta called Helots. They served the Hoplite soldiers also known as the 'Spartiate', the male population of Sparta that was considered 'a citizen soldier' and the elite class. According to Paul Cartledge, professor of Greek history at the University of Cambridge the militaristic society and entire way of life was created and maintained in order to dominate and suppress the Helots (69). One of the reasons the Spartan male population was sent to the Agoge to train "incessantly in preparation for an immediate call to arms" (Cartledge, 69) was because the "Helot underclass were always threatening to rise up in significant numbers against their *masters*" (Cartledge, 69).

The whole Spartan society was crafted around keeping the Helots under their control. The chief magistrates, the Ephors, were tasked, as their first official business to declare *war* against the Helots for a previous revolt that occurred in the 460's BCE. This *war* "meant that any killing of Helots by Spartan citizens, deliberate or otherwise, was officially sanctioned, even perhaps encouraged, and, crucially was in religious terms free from ritual pollution" (Cartledge). At the beginning of every year Spartan pre-adults from the Agoge would be able to show their skill by being a part of this war called the Crypteia. "Plutarch reports that magistrates would select the 'most intelligent' youths and dispatch them into the countryside, with only daggers and basic supplies. It was their mission to slaughter under cover of night every helot they encountered" (Garland). Other Greek citizens looked down upon this harsh treatment of the Helots. Even the Greek philosopher Plato believed that "the helot system was the most controversial example of servitude in Greece" (Cartledge).

The Helot males were forced to work the Spartiates land. They were allowed to keep partial portions of the produce that they reaped to give to their families. The Helot women took care of the children, the cooking, cleaning and the domestic duties of the household. The Helots performed all labors for their masters so that the Spartiates had only one task to perform, their military training.

In the movie, King Leonidas runs into a group of Arcadian soldiers on a hill. Daxos, leader of the Arcadian army questions the Spartans dedication to the fight after noticing the small number of soldiers standing behind Leonidas. "I see I was wrong to expect Sparta's commitment to at least match our own" (Pleavin, Andrew). Leonidas then proceeds to ask a few Arcadian soldiers what their profession is. He receives answers such as Blacksmith, Sculptor and Potter. Leonidas responds, "Spartans! What is your profession?" (Butler, Gerard). The Soldiers respond with three chants of a war cry. This scene is very powerful in the film; it shows Sparta's dedication to the craft of war, but it is just as much subterfuge as the majority of the film. Many of the Spartan soldiers were Helots. They fought and perished at the battle of Thermopylae. The Helots were also in attendance at the Battle of Plataea, but according to the narrator of the film Delios, "Yet they (Persians) stare now across the plain at ten thousand Spartans commanding thirty thousand *free* Greeks!" (Wenham, David). Sparta was not the only Greek city-state to have slaves and they certainly were not the only ones to bring slaves to the battlefield.

Most of the slaves in Greece were procured during war. "They were also bought and sold in a trade market that originated in Asia Minor (Turkey), Scythia (an area that now includes Azerbaijan, Kazakhstan, Ukraine, and southern Russia), and Africa. Slaves represented one-fourth to one-third of the population, or an estimated 80,000-100,000 people" (Driscoll). Over 10,000 slaves were in attendance at the battle of Plataea. According to Peter Hunt in his book, *Slaves, Warfare, and Ideology in the*

Greek historians, "Herodotus wrote that there were seven times more slaves on the battle fields than Spartans" (44).

The filmmakers certainly tried to glorify that the Spartans were free from 'slavery' and that only free men fought, but that has been proven false. Sparta wanted to fight Xerxes for the same reasons Athens, Thebes, Arcadia and all other Greek city-states were fighting, to keep Persia from conquering Greece so the 'elites class and their families' would not be captured by the Persians and made into 'slaves of war' as the Greeks found fit to do to their captives. In the film *300*, Leonidas says to the Ephors, "Sparta will burn! Her men will die at the arms of their women and children will be *slaves* or worse"

The actual 'cause' of the battle of Thermopylae and the fact that all Greek city-states including Sparta had slaves that fought on the battlefields against the Persians, needed to be clarified first and foremost, but there are a few more grievances within the film 300 that still need to be discussed.

Another blatant fallacy in the film is when we see Theron and a Persian messenger showering the diseased Ephors with golden coins. The Ephors were not diseased old men; they were a group of elder Spartans chosen by the Spartiates as magistrates and had power of jurisdiction, but the fallacy is not how they were portrayed visually in the film. It is the fact that the filmmakers tried to assert that Xerxes bribed Theron and the Ephors to gain favor with the counsel. Xerxes did not bribe any Spartans. In the book, *History of Greece*, George Grote wrote, "Xerxes did not rely upon bribes, but upon other different means, for conquering Greece."

Another perversion of the battle can be seen when Leonidas climbs up a mountain to obtain the blessings from the Ephors to go into battle. The Ephors consult the Oracle who states that Sparta must not go to war. As the Ephors final word is law. The filmmakers suggest that Leonidas has become an outlaw by taking 300 of his best men to Thermopylae against their orders. First, Sparta always had two kings. Two of Sparta's most powerful families ruled at the same time. At the time of the Battle, The two kings were Leonidas from the Agiad family and Leotychidas II from the Eurypontid family. Both kings had the right to make decisions in regards to joining the war. Regardless, the Ephors told Leonidas to take soldiers to the 'Hot Gates.' According to the Greek historian Herodotus, "Leonidas had come to Thermopylae, accompanied by the 300 men *which the law assigned him*, whom he had himself chosen from among the citizens, and who were all of them fathers with sons living" (Herodotus and Rawlinson 310). The Ephors assigned just 300 men for two important reasons, the Olympics and the Carneia. The Olympics were celebrated throughout Greece. It was the only time that all Greek city-states would call a truce to their 'civil wars' in order to participate at the games. Sparta soldiers were in attendance at the Olympic games, but the main reason for lack of soldiers to march on Thermopylae was due to the Spartans chief festival, the Carneia that occurred during the same time as the battle. In the film, the Ephor said, "Sparta wages no war at the time of the Carneia" (Kramer, Greg). A statement that was true to historical fact. The Carneia was a religious celebration for the Spartans and it was forbidden that the army leave Sparta during this celebration.

  As pointed out, in this exposition, the film *300* had many similarities to the history of the epic battle, where Leonidas and 7000 men from Greece risked their lives at the pass of Thermopylae to keep the Persian from invading their country. For those that may not know their history, this film can be taken literally and for those that do know their history, it is their responsibility to help separate the truth from fiction. Many people have posted questions on the Internet asking if the film *300* is historically correct. It's good to know that some people would like to know the truth, but there are many others that would rather take the film to be truth. The filmmakers made a wonderful movie, it was intriguing and because it did have so many elements, including actual documented conversations between Xerxes and Leonidas, it gave the audience just a enough truth to make one feel they were actually witnessing history, but just enough fiction to keep it intriguing.

    Stories are often embellished and history is often rewritten. There is nothing wrong with stretching the truth as long as the audience is fully aware of it. The movie *300* was a wonderful visual experience. It was *amazing* how accurate the film was as an overall story, but upon deeper inspection, the film *300* directed by Zack Snyder was merely entertainment and nothing more than that. Let's hope other directors when making films based on historical events keep to the facts and limit the fiction.

Works Cited:

Cartledge, Paul. Thermopylae: the Battle That Changed the World. Woodstock, NY: Overlook, 2006. 69. Print.

O'Connor K. Overview of Ancient Sparta. Ancient Greece: Overview of Ancient Sparta [serial on the Internet]. (2011, Jan), [cited November 24, 2010]; 1. Available from: History Reference Center.

"'300' Trivia: Albino Giants, Sequel Chances — And Sienna Miller - MTV Movie News| MTV." New Music Videos, Reality TV Shows, Celebrity News, Top Stories | MTV. Web. 13 Nov. 2010.

"Sparta." Columbia Electronic Encyclopedia, 6th Edition (2010): 1. Academic Search Complete. EBSCO. Web. 13 Nov. 2010.

300. Dir. Zack Snyder. Perf. David Wenham. Warner Bros., 2006. DVD.
300. Dir. Zack Snyder. Perf. Gerard Butler. Warner Bros., 2006. DVD.
300. Dir. Zack Snyder. Perf. Andrew Pleavin. Warner Bros., 2006. DVD.
300. Dir. Zack Snyder. Perf. Greg Kramer. Warner Bros., 2006. DVD

Foster, Jason K. "Outfoxed AND Outfought." Military History 23.10 (2007): 58-63. World History Collection. EBSCO. Web. 22 Nov. 2010.

"Ancient Greece: The Persian Wars." Washington State University - Pullman, Washington. Web. 22 Nov. 2010.

Cartledge, Paul. "TO DIE FOR?" History Today 52.8 (2002): 19. History Reference Center. EBSCO. Web. 28 Nov. 2010.

Garland, Robert. "MURDER MOST FOUL." History Today 54.2 (2004): 9-15. World

History Collection. EBSCO. Web. 28 Nov. 2010

Driscoll, Sally. "Life as a Slave in Ancient Greece." Ancient Greece: Life as a Slave in Ancient Greece (2011): 1. History Reference Center. EBSCO. Web. 29 Nov. 2010.

Hunt, Peter. Slaves, Warfare, and Ideology in the Greek Historians. Cambridge, U.K.: Cambridge UP, 1998. 44. Print

Grote, George. History of Greece. [Boston, MA]: Elibron Classics, Adamant Media, 2004. 269. Print

Bradford, Ernle Dusgate Selby. The Battle for the West: Thermopylae. New York: McGraw-Hill, 1980. 31. Print.

Herodotus, and George Rawlinson. The Histories. New York: A.A. Knopf, 1997. 263, 314, 310. Print.

YOUR KNOWLEDGE HAS VALUE

- We will publish your bachelor's and
  master's thesis, essays and papers

- Your own eBook and book -
  sold worldwide in all relevant shops

- Earn money with each sale

Upload your text at www.GRIN.com
and publish for free